MONSTER WARS

SEA MONSTERS
vs DRAGONS

SHOWDOWN OF THE LEGENDS

Michael O'Hearn

Consultant:
Michael Delahoyde, PhD

www.raintreepublishers.co.uk
to find out
more information about
Raintree books.

Customers from outside the UK please telephone +44 1865 312262

To order:
☎ Phone 0845 6044371
🖹 Fax +44 (0) 1865 312263
✉ Email myorders@raintreepublishers.co.uk

f Capstone Global Library Limited, a company
incorporated in England and Wales having its registered office at 7 Pilgrim
Street, London EC4V 6LB – Registered company number: 6695882

Text © Capstone Press 2012
First published in the United Kingdom by Capstone Global Library in 2012
The moral rights of the proprietor have been asserted.

Editors: Aaron Sautter and John-Paul Wilkins
Designer: Tracy Davies
Media researcher: Eric Gohl
Production specialist: Eric Manske
Illustrator: Scott Altmann
Originated by Capstone Global Library
Printed and bound in China by South China Printing Company

ISBN 978 1 406 24276 8 (paperback)
16 15 14 13 12
10 9 8 7 6 5 4 3 2 1

Acknowledgements
Alamy/Mary Evans Picture Library, 9; Corbis/Bettmann, 5 (bottom);
iStockphoto/Jack Imes Jr., dragon silhouette; Kobal Collection/Disney/
Paramount, 8; Prominent Features, 10; Shangri-La/Paramount, 11; Walt Disney,
15, 17 (bottom); Newscom/akg-images, 6 (left); Universal Pictures, 17 (top); Walt
Disney Productions/Paramount, 13; Shutterstock/JCElv, 5 (top); Linda Bucklin,
19 (left); lineartestpilot, 6 (right); Ralf Juergen Kraft, sea monster silhouette, 19
(right).

British Library Cataloguing in Publication Data
A full catalogue record for this book is available from the British Library.

CONTENTS

WELCOME TO MONSTER WARS!

It's past midnight. The night is dark. Shadows creep across your bedroom wall. You swear they form a slit-eyed face. Floorboards creak. Trees outside your window groan. It's nothing, you tell yourself. But you lie awake ... watching ... listening ... waiting. You can't help but think a terrifying monster is hiding in your wardrobe.

In these pages, you'll learn the strengths and weaknesses of dragons and sea monsters. And you'll see these brawny beasts face off in a vicious battle. Will the dragon defeat the sea monster with its fiery breath? Or will the sea monster pull the dragon down into the murky ocean depths?

Are monsters real? No. But get ready to watch a truly beastly battle.

THE FRIGHTENING TRUTH:

SEA MONSTER VS DRAGON

★ ★ ★ ★ ★ ★ ★

Tales of dragons are found all around the world. In many European stories, the fearsome beasts often threaten villages and steal treasure. Sometimes they take young women as a **sacrifice**.

In some religious teachings, dragons represent evil. Stories of saints killing dragons show how good has the power to defeat evil. In European **legends**, heroes kill wild dragons to prove their ability as warriors. In Chinese **myths**, however, dragons are often shown as kind creatures that have magical powers.

Stories of fierce sea monsters have been around for thousands of years. In ancient times, fishermen and sailors were often scared of unknown creatures that lived in deep ocean waters. They were terrified that they'd be eaten by a huge, snake-like terror.

Which of these fearsome creatures is more deadly? Read on to learn the dangerous secrets of these massive, mythical monsters!

sacrifice — offering given to a higher being
legend — story passed down through the years that may not be completely true
myth — story told by people in ancient times

SPEED

SEA MONSTER speedy swimmer
★ ★ ★

DRAGON powerful flyer
★ ★ ★ ★ ★

Many dragons live in caves high in the mountains. Most of these dragons can fly at great speed. Flying is essential for attacking towns and castles. Dragons have great, leathery wings similar to those of bats. They speed through the sky with powerful thrusts of their wings to hunt for **prey**.

prey — animal that is hunted by another animal for food

Sea monsters are expert swimmers. Some slither through the water like snakes. Others have bodies or tails like fish. These monsters can swim incredibly fast beneath the water.

A few legendary sea monsters, such as the Kraken, are so huge that they let their prey come to them. Sailors might sail their ships right over the gaping jaws of the gigantic beast. They would not realize the danger until it was too late.

FRIGHTFUL FACT

Chinese dragons usually have no wings or very small wings. But many can still fly with magic.

SIZE

SEA MONSTER massive giants

★ ★ ★ ★ ★

DRAGON huge flying beasts

★ ★ ★

Sea monsters may be the largest of all mythical creatures. The Leviathan was a sea monster from the Bible. It was said to have seven heads, 300 eyes, and was over 1,450 kilometres (900 miles) long. The legendary Kraken, with its long and deadly tentacles, was believed to stretch up to 2.4 kilometres (1.5 miles) wide. One Scottish myth tells of a sea monster so large it could swallow several whales whole – in one gulp!

Dragons can't compete with sea monsters in sheer size. But they are among the largest monsters to live on land. According to one Greek legend, dragons in Africa measured 18 metres (60 feet) long. One American Indian myth describes a dragon's mouth being as big as a large cave.

FRIGHTFUL FACT

Dragons are famous for their large **appetites**, as well as their size. Smaug, the dragon in the book *The Hobbit*, ate several fat ponies in one meal.

DRAGON ATTACK STYLE

DRAGON fire, claws, and teeth

★ ★ ★ ★ ★

Many dragons breathe out terrible blasts of fire to attack enemies. These fire-breathing monsters can destroy whole villages and armies with great speed. Some dragons use different breath weapons. They might use deadly blasts of ice, acid, or even poison.

Dragons also use other deadly weapons in combat. In a close fight, a dragon can use its razor-sharp claws to slash at its enemy. Or it can deal a deadly bite with its powerful jaws, lined with sharp, jagged teeth. Dragons can also bash and stun enemies with their strong, whip-like tails. Some dragons have spiked tails that can cause serious wounds.

FRIGHTFUL FACT

The word "dragon" comes from the Greek word *Draken*, which means "to watch". In many legends dragons are guardians, or watchers, of valuable treasures.

SEA MONSTER ATTACK STYLE

SEA MONSTER powerful tentacles
★ ★ ★ ★

Sea monsters use a variety of attacks. Sea serpents often hunt for ships sailing far from shore to feed on sailors. They coil their bodies around unsuspecting ships to crush them. Then they devour the sailors as they fall into the sea.

The gigantic Kraken waits for a ship to pass by. Then it grabs the ship with its huge **tentacles**. The beast pulls the ship down into the icy water and drags helpless sailors into its gaping mouth.

In one European legend, a sea monster had a long, pointed horn on its head. It used the horn to pierce the bottom of ships, causing them to sink. Then it collected the crew as a tasty prize.

tentacles — long, flexible arms

WEAKNESSES

To slay a dragon, a hero has to first find its weakness. In the book *The Hobbit*, the dragon Smaug is killed by a single arrow through a missing scale on its belly. In a famous German legend, the hero Sigurd kills the dragon Fafnir. He first digs a ditch and hides in it. Then he attacks the dragon's soft belly as it crawls over the ditch. The famous English Dragon of Wantley is killed when it falls on the hero's spiked suit of armour.

Gigantic sea monsters have no obvious weaknesses. But powerful sea monsters can be defeated if a hero is clever and courageous. In one Japanese tale, a woman kills a huge sea monster with only a knife. She first stabs the creature's eyes. The blind beast then can't defend itself as the woman finishes the job.

SEA MONSTER easily outwitted
★

DRAGON soft underbelly
★ ★

FRIGHTFUL FACT

According to some legends, drinking or bathing in dragon blood can give a person magical strength and wisdom.

GET READY TO RUMBLE!

The water churns and the sea glows red with flames. The ocean has become a battle zone. The king of the deep sea is ready to protect its watery turf. And the fiery king of the sky is prepared to show its power. But there's room for only one ruler here. Only one beast can win this battle. The other will pay the ultimate price for defeat.

You might want to turn your ship around, but keep reading. You get to watch this battle from the main deck. It's sea versus sky in this fearsome fight to the finish!

SEA MONSTER

SPEED	SIZE	ATTACK STYLE	WEAKNESS
★★★	★★★★★	★★★★	★

DRAGON

SPEED	SIZE	ATTACK STYLE	WEAKNESS
★★★★★	★★★	★★★★★	★★

ONE LAST THING ...

The following battle is based on creatures from legends and stories. Dragons don't soar overhead or blast fire from their mouths. And huge sea creatures don't pull ships under the water to eat the crew. However, you can still imagine how these monsters might fight each other. So dim the lights, turn the page, and get ready for a fierce, beastly battle!

DEADLY DUEL

★ ★ ★ ★ ★ ★

A driving wind pushes dark clouds across the grey sky. The clouds' wide shadows slide over the choppy sea below. Waves pound the cliff face rising from the shore.

A red beast soars over the ocean. Its snout is long and flat with wicked teeth. Its green eyes are wide and bright. Its long neck is connected to a scaly body with a long, spiked tail. Broad, leathery wings stretch from the creature's back and drive it through the air. In its front claws, it holds the limp body of a dead goat.

The dragon flies through an opening in the cliff wall. The cave is dark, but gold and jewels glitter in the dim light. The dragon sniffs the air and scans the cave. Satisfied that its treasure is safe, the creature settles on the floor with the dead goat.

The dragon tears off chunks of meat and chomps the bones. Suddenly it stops to sniff the air. The dragon turns and sees a long, slimy tentacle stretching towards its meal.

The tentacle slithers forward and curls around the leg of the goat. The dragon opens its mouth and a thin stream of fire stings the grey intruder. The tentacle snakes backwards, then springs forward with surprising speed.

It coils around the dragon's neck, squeezing tightly. The dragon opens its mouth, but no fire comes out. It slashes and cuts the tentacle with its sharp front claws. Black blood oozes from the deep cuts.

Despite the wounds, the tentacle squeezes the dragon even tighter. It jerks backwards and drags the red beast towards the cave opening. The dragon digs its claws into the floor, leaving long deep scratches in the stone. But it can't resist the overpowering tentacle.

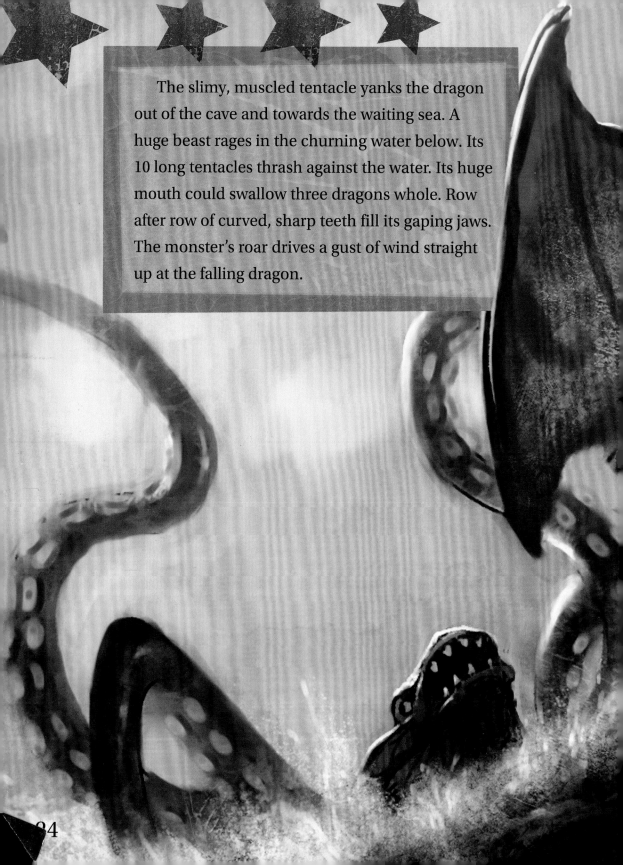

The slimy, muscled tentacle yanks the dragon out of the cave and towards the waiting sea. A huge beast rages in the churning water below. Its 10 long tentacles thrash against the water. Its huge mouth could swallow three dragons whole. Row after row of curved, sharp teeth fill its gaping jaws. The monster's roar drives a gust of wind straight up at the falling dragon.

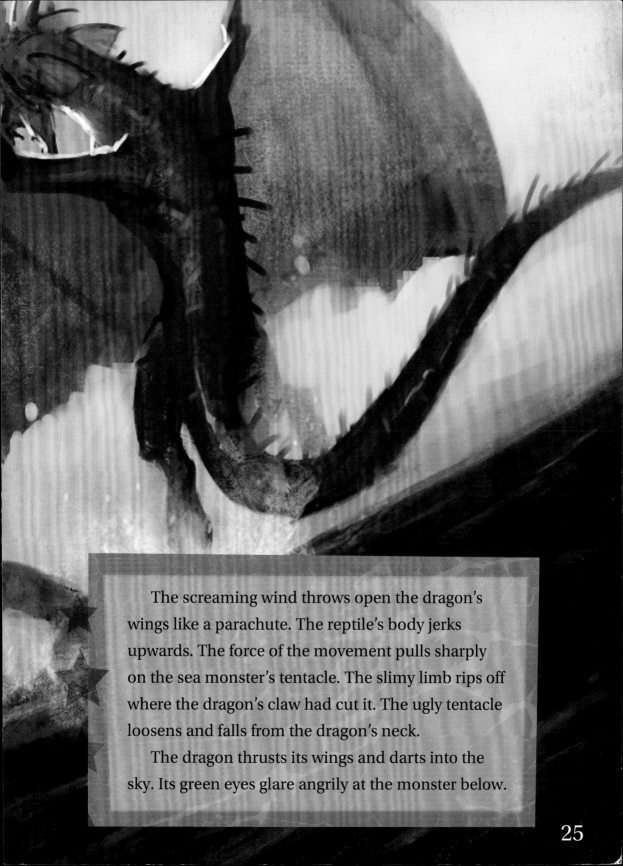

The screaming wind throws open the dragon's wings like a parachute. The reptile's body jerks upwards. The force of the movement pulls sharply on the sea monster's tentacle. The slimy limb rips off where the dragon's claw had cut it. The ugly tentacle loosens and falls from the dragon's neck.

The dragon thrusts its wings and darts into the sky. Its green eyes glare angrily at the monster below.

The dragon shrieks and dives towards the sea. It tucks in its wings, and its body goes rigid like an arrow. It streaks towards its enemy – a red blur against the grey sky. The dragon blasts a stream of fire at the sea monster.

The intense fire overwhelms the beast. It bellows in pain and dives below the water's surface. The waves glow red under the dragon's fire. The water bubbles and churns from the heat. The dragon levels off and holds its breath. Its green eyes scan the water.

The sea monster lies below the flaming surface. When the flames die down, it snakes its powerful tentacles out of the water to grab its enemy. But the dragon flies smoothly between the flailing arms. Then it turns and blows a scorching ball of flame at one of the tentacles. The charred limb turns black and falls limply to the sea.

The sea monster leaps out of the flaming water and snaps its jaws at the dragon. The flying beast dodges the bite, but a thrashing tentacle clips its wing. The dragon tumbles through the sky and crashes into the water.

More tentacles snake across the water to grip the winged creature. The dragon whips its spiked tail and spears one tentacle. It scorches two more with its fiery breath. But the other tentacles pull the dragon towards the sea monster's deadly teeth.

The furious dragon snaps its tail again. The spiked tail slices a long, bloody wound in the sea monster's grey flesh. The dragon tries to blast fire at his enemy's eyes and mouth. But the monster's wild tentacles are wrapped tightly around the dragon. They violently pull the shrieking dragon into the sea monster's hungry mouth. Its jaws slam shut, silencing its prey. Blood trickles from the sea monster's mouth. It roars in victory, then sinks back into the deep, dark sea.

GLOSSARY

appetite desire for food or drink

legend story passed down through the years that may not be completely true

myth story told by people in ancient times. Myths often tried to explain natural events.

prey animal that is hunted by another animal for food

sacrifice offering, such as a person or treasure, given to a higher being

tentacles long, flexible arms of some ocean animals that are used to touch, grab, or smell

FIND OUT MORE

BOOKS

Dragons (Monster Chronicles), Stephen Krensky (Lerner, 2008)

Field Guide to Dragons, Amanda Wood (Templar Publishing, 2007)

Monsterology, Dugald Steer (Templar Publishing, 2008)

Mysteries of Water Monsters (Unsolved!), Kathryn Walker (Crabtree Publishing, 2008)

WEBSITES

www.draconika.com/index.php
Find out all you ever wanted to know about dragons on this website.

www.polenth.com
There are plenty of dragon activities on this website, including quizzes, a wordsearch, and even a dragon name generator!

INDEX